Hanukkah /
39878005885532

Hanukkah

by Lola M. Schaefer

Consulting Editor: Gail Saunders-Smith, Ph.D.

Consultant: Dr. Aryeh Cohen
Chairman, Department of Jewish Studies
University of Judaism, Los Angeles

Pebble Books

an imprint of Capstone Press
Mankato, Minnesota

Pebble Books are published by Capstone Press
151 Good Counsel Drive, P.O. Box 669, Mankato, Minnesota 56002
http://www.capstone-press.com

1 2 3 4 5 6 06 05 04 03 02 01

Library of Congress Cataloging-in-Publication Data
Schaefer, Lola M., 1950–
    Hanukkah/by Lola M. Schaefer.
    p. cm.—(Holidays and celebrations)
    Includes bibliographical references and index.
    Summary: Presents, in simple text and photographs, the history of Hanukkah
and how it is celebrated in the United States.
    ISBN 0-7368-0662-8
    1. Hanukkah—Juvenile literature. [1. Hanukkah. 2. Holidays.] I. Title.
II. Series.
BM695.H3 S27 2001
394.267—dc21
                                                                    00-023056

Note to Parents and Teachers

The Holidays and Celebrations series supports national social studies standards related to culture. This book describes Hanukkah and illustrates how it is celebrated in the United States. The photographs support early readers in understanding the text. The repetition of words and phrases helps early readers learn new words. This book also introduces early readers to subject-specific vocabulary words, which are defined in the Words to Know section. Early readers may need assistance to read some words and to use the Table of Contents, Words to Know, Read More, Internet Sites, and Index/Word List sections of the book.

Table of Contents

Hanukkah is a Jewish holiday. It celebrates a victory and a miracle.

People celebrate Hanukkah during the Jewish month of Kislev. The celebration lasts for eight days in November or December.

8

Hanukkah celebrates a Jewish victory more than 2,000 years ago. Enemies wanted to destroy the Jewish religion. They ruined the only Temple where Jewish people prayed. The Jewish people fought their enemies and won.

The Jewish people fixed the Temple. They could now worship there. They looked for pure oil to light the lamps in the Temple. They found enough pure oil to last one day. It was a miracle when the oil burned for eight days.

Jewish people light a menorah during Hanukkah. The menorah celebrates the miracle of light. Hanukkah sometimes is called the Festival of Lights.

Jewish people light one candle for each of the eight nights of Hanukkah. They put the menorah in a window to tell others about Hanukkah.

Jewish people say prayers while they light the menorah. Some people sing songs and give gifts.

Families and friends gather to eat special foods during Hanukkah. Children play a game called dreidl.

Some Jewish people light a menorah in their synagogue during Hanukkah. They say special prayers of thanks to God.

dreidl—a spinning top with four sides; each side of the dreidl has one Hebrew letter; the letters mean "A great miracle happened there."

holiday—a day to celebrate an event or to honor a person

Kislev—the third month of the ancient Hebrew calendar; Kislev is in November or December.

menorah—a candle holder; menorahs for Hanukkah hold nine candles; the ninth candle is used to light the eight candles of Hanukkah.

synagogue—a building where Jewish people come together to pray

Temple—the building in Jerusalem where all Jewish people gathered to worship God

worship—to show love and commitment to God or a god

Read More

Clark, Anne, David Rose and Gill Rose. *Hanukkah.* A World of Holidays. Austin, Texas: Raintree Steck-Vaughn, 1998.

Fishman, Cathy Goldberg. *On Hanukkah.* New York: Atheneum Books for Young Readers, 1998.

Hoyt-Goldsmith, Diane. *Celebrating Hanukkah.* New York: Holiday House, 1996.

Ziefert, Harriet. *Eight Days of Hanukkah: A Holiday Step Book.* New York: Viking Books, 1997.

Internet Sites

About Hanukkah
http://rats2u.com/christmas/hanukkah_index.htm

Celebrating Hanukkah
http://www.kidskourt.com/Holidays/HanCelebrate.htm

Chanukah on the Net
http://www.holidays.net/chanukah

Hanukkah
http://www.joi.org/celebrate/hanuk

Index/Word List

Word Count: 206
Early-Intervention Level: 14

Editorial Credits

Mari C. Schuh, editor; Heather Kindseth, designer; Kimberly Danger and Heidi Schoof, photo researchers

Photo Credits

Corbis, 8, 10
David F. Clobes, 4, 12, 14, 16, 18 (both), 20
Index Stock Imagery, cover
International Stock/Patrick Ramsey, 1
Richard B. Levine, 6

24